WHAT about & the WOMAN?

God's Revelation Concerning Women

Bishop C.L. Long

Treasure House

An Imprint of

Destiny Image® Publishers, Inc.

P.O. Box 310
Shippensburg, PA 17257-0310

"For where your treasure is,
there will your heart be also." Matthew 6:21

ISBN 1-56043-312-4

For Worldwide Distribution
Printed in the U.S.A.

This book and all other Destiny Image, Revival Press,
and Treasure House books are available
at Christian bookstores and distributors worldwide.

For a U.S. bookstore nearest you, call **1-800-722-6774**.
For more information on foreign distributors, call **717-532-3040**.
Or reach us on the Internet: **http://www.reapernet.com**

Dedication

This book is lovingly dedicated to the memory of my parents, the late Mason and Pauline Long, without whose financial support the Scripture Cathedral ministry would not have been possible. With a humble heart I acknowledge their financial contribution, as well as their staunch spiritual and emotional support.

God, in His infinite wisdom, called my father home on April 4, 1978. Sixteen years later, on December 25, 1994, He also called my mother from labor to reward. My parents' role in my personal and professional life was special and unique. I loved them deeply. Their memories are like my heartbeat and will be with me for an eternity.

Acknowledgments

Many people have directly and/or indirectly contributed to the writing of this book. I am infinitely grateful to my three devoted children—Clarence, Edward, and Chantel—who, through their unconditional love and support, have taught me about faith, trust, and the things that really matter in life.

Words are an inadequate vehicle in expressing my sincere appreciation to my wife of 37 years, JoAnne, who has stood by my side with unquestionable loyalty. She possesses the innate ability of saying and doing the right thing at the right time. Her encouragement coupled with her belief in my abilities enabled me to complete this work. Thank you, honey.

Contents

Foreword

As a woman of God, nothing saddens me more than to see the masses of women who have not received abundant prosperity, healing, and spiritual greatness because of their inability to believe that such is the perfect will of God concerning them. Their unbelief evolves from misconception and misinterpretation of the Word of God, which has been predominantly instilled in their minds through years of (sometimes unintentionally and sometimes intentionally) erroneous, manipulative teaching of men and women who sought to control the Body of Christ and enhance Christianity through traditionalism.

This traditional curse, caused by man's focus on primitive religious/cultural practices, has impeded the growth of the Church, the uniting of the Body of Christ, and the individual Christian liberty for women. For years, God's people have feuded over dress codes, hairstyles, and other trivial doctrinal issues. For this reason, the Church has missed the very essence of God's desire and ability to provide a more excellent life to the believer and a more effective ministry to the world.

What About the Woman? is a Christian road map to spiritual freedom and rebirth. After three decades of traditional pastoring, Bishop C.L. Long has dared to come forth to speak the truth of God's revelation to him concerning "the woman." This magnificent unfolding of God's revelation preludes the promised anointing soon to descend upon the Church. Many religious leaders will criticize this truth because tradition and doctrine are "man's power" of rulership over God's people.

Others who have been praying for conflict resolution and answers to their concerns about women will rejoice that their prayers have been answered and join the ranks of God's flock experiencing liberty in Christ Jesus.

As this watchman on the wall has taken deliberate charge over his post, we rejoice in his obedience to God, to the revelation given by God, and to the leading of the Holy Spirit that will strengthen him to endure all things through Christ, as we strive to become a model of the twenty-first century Church.

Minister Sharon Hamm
Cathedral Ministries, Inc.
Washington, D.C.

Preface

Let your women keep silence in the churches: for it is not permitted unto them to speak; but they are commanded to be under obedience, as also saith the law. And if they will learn any thing, let them ask their husbands at home: for it is a shame for women to speak in the church. What? came the word of God out from you? or came it unto you only? (1 Corinthians 14:34-36)

Let the woman learn in silence with all subjection. But I suffer not a woman to teach, nor to usurp authority over the man, but to be in silence (1 Timothy 2:11-12).

These words from the Epistles of Paul have been a source of perplexity to lovers of the Word of God—in particular, to the great and growing company of women who feel a fire burning in their souls that they cannot smother and who know that the hand of God has been laid upon them for service.

In the whole of Christendom, women have been forbidden to teach, preach, or even to offer audible prayer in church, based on these Scriptures. Many conservative denominations allow the women to take on only a very small part of the work of the ministry.

Now, some people would simply brush aside the words from the Epistles of Paul by declaring that Paul was merely expressing his own fallible opinion. However, I believe, in expressing this opinion, that Paul is writing under the inspiration of the Spirit of God. In fact, Paul goes on to follow First Corinthians 14:34-36 with these words: "If any man think himself to be a prophet, or spiritual, let him acknowledge that the things that I write unto you are the commandments of the Lord. But if any man be ignorant, let him be ignorant" (1 Cor. 14:37-38). I do not seek to brush aside the apostle's writings, but rather to genuinely *understand them* in the light of proper biblical context, proven of methodology, interpretation, and the cultural context of Paul's day as it may be accurately compared to ours.

Introduction

I find it interesting that the passage of Scripture in which the apostle Paul "commands women to keep silence in the churches" is found in chapter 14 of First Corinthians—the same chapter that many call "the great Pentecostal chapter."

Tell me, who has ever seen a Pentecostal church where the women kept silence and were not permitted to speak? I haven't, nor do I know of any church other than the Pentecostal church where women are permitted to speak freely. In the Pentecostal church you find men, women, boys, and girls alike studying the Word of God in preparation for end-time ministry service as missionaries, evangelists, and preachers.

However, if you just skim over the surface of these Scripture passages without detailed study, it would "seem" that the custom in the Pentecostal/apostolic church today is at variance with the teachings of the apostle Paul. Therefore, it is incumbent upon each of us to either admit that we ignore and violate the Word of God in this particular instance, or we must interpret it in harmony with the practices that we permit in our midst. May the following chapters help guide you through a fresh study of God's Word and heart concerning women in the Church and His Kingdom.

Chapter 1

Keep Your Face to the Wind!

On July 10, 1988, the Holy Spirit suddenly visited me as I lay awake in bed, and the irrefutable voice of God spoke to me and said, "Clarence, get up!" I immediately responded to His voice and rose from my bed. He directed me to get dressed, to get in my car, and to drive until He told me to stop. I knew that I had a divine appointment with God that would somehow change my life.

As a pastor, I had been wrestling with the question, "What about the woman?" for two decades prior to that fateful morning. The tension created by my unspoken and unanswered questions concerning the traditional limitations placed on women in the church had begun to take its toll in the form of chronic insomnia. It was becoming obvious to me that the traditions of man were in direct conflict with the truths in God's Word. To make matters worse, truth was borne out by the genuine ministries of women chronicled over multiplied centuries of Church history. I knew the answer to the question, but I wasn't sure what to do about it.

The problem went all the way back to my early years when, as a rebellious youngster, I refused to submit to authority and thought that I "knew everything." When I accepted Jesus Christ as Savior and Lord of my life, I was overwhelmed by my condition as a sinner and experienced an immediate transformation. I gave up every idea about "knowing everything" and was suddenly consumed with a zest for knowledge and a willingness to live a subservient life totally devoted and submitted to Christ.

When I joined the church where I had been saved, it never occurred to me to question the authority of my pastor. I had given up my rebellious ways, and I knew that my spiritual mentor had been a charter member of his particular religious organization—an organization that had been founded many years before my birth.

As a result, when I accepted my call into the ministry, it just seemed natural that I, too, would follow in my pastor's footsteps and become a member of this organization as well. So it was that in 1961, when I accepted my first pastorate, I joined this organization and followed its leadership—*and doctrines*—without question.

As I grew in the knowledge of the Lord, I encountered issues that I did not understand. I noticed that my church organization set forth rules that didn't seem to be supported by the Scriptures, but I summarily repressed the questions that came to mind because I didn't want to step back into the rebellious ways of my youth and bring dishonor to God.

The problem was that God wouldn't allow these issues to go away. He began to deal with me about the unanswered questions that I had refused to ask publicly. His main focus was on the issue of "women preachers," but I was also wrestling with side issues concerning the outward appearance of women, such as makeup, the cutting of hair, and the wearing of pants. I had faithfully served as a pastor for over three decades within a church organization that strictly forbade all four of these things! There would be no women preachers, no makeup, no cutting of the hair, and no women in pants in our churches. What was God doing to me now? Was He calling me to step into rebellion once again?

When God ordered me out of bed and into my car, I didn't hesitate to obey. Although I didn't have a clue about where I was going, I knew emphatically that I was being directed by God. So I drove for the better part of the morning until 9:00 a.m. when the Lord told me to stop and park my car in an isolated area in North Carolina, hundreds of miles away from my warm bed in Washington, D.C. I got out of my car and began to walk, anticipating God's next directive all the while.

A Divine Response

My walk came to an abrupt end when God's effervescent presence overwhelmed me and His shekinah glory encapsulated my very being. He said, "Turn to the wind." When I turned my face to the wind, God said, *"I'll blow the hell out of you, but if you turn your back to the wind, I will blow you out of the way."* I knew what He was talking about, and from that moment on, I did not question His divine will. I knew that in all likelihood, I would lose church members who would neither understand nor accept this new revelation about "the woman."

For years I had allowed myself to remain stagnant, though I knew the voice of God was calling me to step out on the stormy waters of controversy at His command. But I was no longer willing to be imprisoned by fear. I returned to my car and began to retrace the miles of the long drive home. But I was not the same man who had passed that way in the early morning hours. A transformation had taken place, and through God's divine providence, I was free! I was determined to proclaim my freedom and walk in this new independence, despite the fact that I knew it would come at a cost.

When I finally reached Washington, D.C., I immediately contacted my attorney and told him to draft a letter of resignation from my organization. That day I became the President and Presiding Prelate over a new organization, "The Cathedral Ministries, Inc." From the onset, I was met with opposition, but I was prepared for the conflict in advance by the Spirit of the Lord, who took me to the Book of Habakkuk where the prophet declared, "...Write the vision, and make it plain..." (Hab. 2:2). Nothing and no one would deter me from my quest to fulfill the vision I'd received that morning in North Carolina.

Over the years, I had been entrusted with many "mothers" in my church who were old enough to be my physical mother or grandmother. This powerful army of prayer warriors had faithfully prayed me through many adverse situations in my life and ministry, and they had constantly offered their staunch support, both financially and emotionally, over the years. God let me know that He was going to call many of these faithful mothers to their heavenly reward in the years that would follow that visitation of 1988. Yet He also assured me that for every one of these precious saints whom He called home, He would send ten more who would readily accept this revelation about the role of women in the

Church of Jesus Christ and would faithfully work with me in its fulfillment. God has been faithful to His spoken word to me.

I will never forget the month of June in 1997, when we made history by finally sponsoring the first Annual Women's Conference of The Scripture Cathedral. This conference marked the public manifestation of a decade of labor, love, and sacrifice on behalf of God's command to release women to fulfill their God-given ministry call. Prior to this, women who ministered in my parish were only allowed to address the congregation from a podium on the lower level. This was simply "the way it was done" in every pulpit represented by my previous church association. Finally, God had His way.

Heaven watched as female ministers were invited to the pulpit and were addressed by their title of Minister or Evangelist—not simply by the term Missionary (which supposedly represented a lower level of anointing and authority). Evangelist Ivory Bostic was among this elite group of women who had ministered many times, but never in my pulpit. It was befitting that she would be the one chosen to set the stage for the manifestation of this new revelation. Many more were to follow her, including my wife, JoAnne, who preached her debut sermon only a year ago along with Sharon Hamm.

I delight in the Lord's mercy and grace, for He has been faithful despite my reluctance to heed His voice. Today I can say, "It is the Lord's doing, and it is marvellous in our eyes" (see Mk. 12:10). To God be the glory.

Did Paul Hate Women?

But what of the preachers and others in the Church world who advance the theory that Paul did not like women? "After all," they say, "that great apostle never married, and he was, in fact, a woman-hater." It is obvious to them that this is the only explanation for the restrictions that he placed on women in his writings. It is time to set the record straight. I propose to you that Paul was not a *woman-hater*, nor did he advise celibacy as some would have you believe. He gave this advice primarily because of the dire circumstances of impending persecution and death by martyrdom that existed in his day. If you find this hard to accept, then examine the context of Paul's statement in the Book of First Corinthians:

> *Now concerning virgins I have no commandment of the Lord: yet I give my judgment, as one that hath obtained mercy of the Lord to be faithful. I suppose therefore that this is good for the present distress, I say, that it is good for a man so to be. Art thou bound unto a wife? seek not to be loosed. Art thou loosed from a wife? seek not a wife. But and if thou marry, thou hast not sinned; and if a virgin marry, she hath not sinned. Nevertheless such shall have trouble in the flesh: but I spare you. But this I say, brethren, the time is short: it remaineth, that both they that have wives be as though they had none; and they that weep, as though they wept not; and they that rejoice, as though they rejoiced not; and they that buy, as though they possessed not* (1 Corinthians 7:25-30).

Paul advised celibacy because of what he called the "present distress" (see 1 Cor. 7:26), referring to the persecutions and afflictions to which Christians in his time were exposed. He goes on in verses 31 through 40 to describe the advantages of unmarried persons who are free to devote themselves wholeheartedly to the service of the Lord. Yet if one thing is clear from this passage, it is that the apostle Paul was not against matrimony. The Book of Hebrews reinforces the New Testament stance on marriage where it says, "Marriage is honourable in all, and the bed undefiled" (Heb. 13:4a).

If Paul did indeed hate women and despised the institution of marriage, then why did he give both such prominent positions in his requirements and qualifications for candidates to the offices of bishop, pastor, and deacon?

This is a true saying, If a man desire the office of a bishop, he desireth a good work. A bishop then must be blameless, the husband of one wife, vigilant, sober, of good behaviour, given to hospitality, apt to teach; not given to wine, no striker, not greedy of filthy lucre; but patient, not a brawler, not covetous; one that ruleth well his own house, having his children in subjection with all gravity; (for if a man know not how to rule his own house, how shall he take care of the church of God?) not a novice, lest being lifted up with pride he fall into the condemnation of the devil. Moreover he must have a good report of them which are without; lest he fall into reproach and the snare of the devil. Likewise must the deacons be grave, not doubletongued, not given to much wine, not greedy of filthy lucre; holding the mystery of the faith in a pure conscience. And let these also first be proved; then let them use the office of a deacon, being found blameless. Even so must their wives be grave, not slanderers, sober, faithful in all things. Let the deacons be the husbands of one wife, ruling their children and their own houses well. For they that have used the office of a deacon well purchase to themselves a good degree, and great boldness in the faith which is in Christ Jesus (1 Timothy 3:1-13).

For this cause left I thee in Crete, that thou shouldest set in order the things that are wanting, and ordain elders in every city, as I had appointed thee: If any be blameless, the husband of one wife, having faithful children not accused of riot or unruly. For a bishop must be blameless, as the steward of God; not self-willed, not soon angry, not given to wine, no striker, not given to filthy lucre; but a lover of hospitality, a lover of good men, sober, just, holy, temperate; holding fast the faithful word as he hath been taught, that he may be able by sound doctrine both to exhort and to convince the gainsayers (Titus 1:5-9).

Now if the apostle Paul hated women or felt that all ministers should be celibate, would it not stand to reason he would have advised Timothy and Titus to find unmarried men for this most responsible position? Yet it is obvious that he did neither.

Paul spoke in terms that publicly demonstrated his high regard for womanhood and for the work of women in the ministry:

I commend unto you Phebe our sister, which is a servant of the church which is an Cenchrea: that ye receive her in the Lord, as becometh saints, and that ye assist her in whatsoever business she hath need of you: for she hath been a succourer of many, and of myself also (Romans 16:1-2).

Paul considered Phebe to be a very important woman in the church at Rome. Notice the language the apostle used in his letter to the Roman believers (including the men in that local body): "I *commend* unto you Phebe...*receive* her...assist her in *whatsoever business* she hath need of you...." In other words, don't just push Phebe aside and take over, but assist her in whatever business she has need of you. In his warm greetings, Paul does not forget the women in Rome.

Greet Priscilla and Aquila my helpers in Christ Jesus: who have for my life laid down their own necks: unto whom not only I give thanks, but also all the churches of the Gentiles (Romans 16:3-4).

Paul defied the customs of his day—and even the "modern" custom of our day—when he addressed the wife, Priscilla, *before* mentioning her husband, Aquila. This doesn't sound like the work of a woman-hater, a sexist, or a male chauvinist. In verse 6 he wrote, "Greet Mary, who bestowed much labour on us" (Rom. 16:6).

Salute Tryphena and Tryphosa, who labour in the Lord. Salute the beloved Persis, which laboured much in the Lord (Romans 16:12).

From the Greek we know that these three individuals were women. And since Paul said Tryphena and Tryphosa "labour[ed] in the Lord," and that Persis "laboured much in the Lord," I believe there is no doubt that these women had some kind of ministry.

In an extensive passage to the church at Ephesus, Paul illustrates how the husband-wife relationship depicts the relationship between Christ and the Church, and he uses the occasion to exhort the husbands to love their wives.

Husbands, love your wives, even as Christ also loved the church, and gave Himself for it; that He might sanctify and cleanse it with the washing of water by the word, that He might present it to Himself a glorious church, not having spot, or wrinkle, or any such thing; but that it should be holy and without blemish. So ought men to love their wives as their own bodies. He that loveth his wife loveth himself. For no man ever yet hated his own flesh; but nourisheth and cherisheth it, even as the Lord the church: for we are members of His body, of His flesh, and of His bones. For this cause shall a man leave his father and mother, and shall be joined unto his wife, and they two shall be one flesh. This is a great mystery: but I speak concerning Christ and the church. Nevertheless let every one of you in particular so love his wife even as himself; and the wife see that she reverence her husband (Ephesians 5:25-33).

In Colossians 3:19, Paul wrote, "Husbands, love your wives, and be not bitter against them." Are these the words of a woman-hater? Certainly not! On the contrary, they show this great apostle, though denied the sweet refining and inspiring influence, comradeship, and companionship of a godly wife, highly esteemed good women as well as good men.

If, indeed, men would heed Paul's counsel, then most of the sorrow and woes of good wives would disappear! Jesus' attitude toward women is an example to all men. No one could ever treat women with greater consideration than did the Lord Jesus Christ. It is time for every man who calls upon the name of Christ to model his ways and conduct after the example of Jesus Christ Himself.

Chapter 2

Is the Man the Head of the Woman?

Throughout the Church world today and in the past, various male leaders seemed to have made it their mission in life to be hard on women. (Only God knows whether they have done this out of fear, personal insecurity, vindictive male chauvinism, or sheer ignorance.) Many preachers and husbands who call themselves Christians are just "hard," period. You can spot them by their fruits.

These are the men who act and talk like their wives are their own God-given doormats and personal slaves. Whether they are hidden behind closed doors at home or strutting through the foyer of their local church, they walk all over the women in their lives most of the time. Figuratively speaking, these men have a foot "firmly planted on the necks" of their wives and children. Given the opportunity, they will try to exert their domineering will on any woman unfortunate enough to be nearby as well! If anyone dares to challenge their behavior and their extremely controlling ways, they will puff up their chests and declare,

"Don't you know the Bible says the man is the head of the woman? Read your Bible, man!"

What Does the Word Say?

Is the man the head of the woman? On the surface, this seems to be implied in the following Scripture passage from the Book of First Corinthians: "But I would have you know, that the head of every man is Christ; and the head of the woman is the man; and the head of Christ is God" (1 Cor. 11:3).

The first question concerns the phrase translated in the Authorized Version as "the head of the woman is the man." As good as this revered translation is, it does have some serious limitations from time to time and place to place, and this is one of those times and places. If you look at this Scripture passage in some newer translations using more modern English terms, you will quickly realize that Paul's statement in the Book of First Corinthians is actually in perfect agreement with his statement in Ephesians 5:23, which says, "For the husband is the head of the wife, even as Christ is the head of the church: and He is the saviour of the body."

I would have you know, however, that of every man Christ is the head, that the head of a woman is her husband, and that the head of Christ is God (1 Corinthians 11:3 Weymouth).

But I wish you to know the head of the woman is the husband, and the head of Christ is God (1 Corinthians 11:3 Worrell).

Now let me ask the question again: "Is the man the head of every woman?" No! A man may be "the head" of one woman...his wife. He is not the head of every woman. And even this "headship" has some major surprises for the uninformed!

This dynasty of male domination has been preserved and handed down from generation to generation by preachers who like to just skim over the top of the Scriptures, almost as if they were "panning" for gold. Yet even in gold fields, the only real wealth comes from the deep veins of precious metal. In other words, you have to dig down into the Word of God if you really want to find out what God says about any given subject. Halfhearted, half-baked scholarship and discernment do to the human soul what half-baked food does to the natural stomach—it produces heartburn and possibly more serious and life-threatening illnesses.

There are some things that I preach from my pulpit under God's direction that I know full well my people won't want to accept, but I preach them anyway. But this is different from the silly things some ministers fuss and fight over—things that the Scriptures don't really support anyway. One preacher tried to impress me with the same old claim one time, "Bishop, the man is the head of the woman." I knew what he meant, and better yet, I knew what the Bible context meant. So I shook my head and said, "No, no. Men are not above women in the Lord. If that was the case, women could never be saved unless the men around them gave them permission!" This kind of attitude is pervasive, and at times, it gets downright intrusive in the lives of sincere believers in countless local churches.

I've had guest preachers come to Scripture Cathedral and try to tell every woman in the house of God how to dress—*including my wife!* In the first place, no preacher or any other man is over my wife—I am. And while we are on the subject, I want to tell every preacher out there, "It is none of your business whatsoever how my wife dresses. *That's my business.* How my wife wears her hair is none of your business either, nor is it the business of any other man in the church or any other preacher anywhere. It is my business. She wears her hair to suit me, not you. She dresses to suit me, not you. If your wife wants to put up with your idiosyncrasy, that's her problem, but don't try to push that off on my wife."

I told one minister who wanted to bring a lot of this kind of foolishness into the church, "Don't bring that mess into this church. As pastor, I am the head of our local church body. While Jesus is the head of the Church universally, He has placed me at the gate of Scripture Cathedral as His undershepherd. That is why I have authority here. (Government is in the office of pastor.) So don't say another word about the 'woman business' while you're here."

The original Greek word translated variously as "man" or "husband" in the New Testament is *aner*. The common Greek of the New Testament era didn't have a specific word for husband or for a married man. Likewise, the Greek term *gyne* was used interchangeably for both wife and woman. The only way to determine the proper English term is through context and setting. For instance, you must tell from the context whether the writer is talking about women in general, or whether he is talking strictly about wives or women within the marriage covenant.

Our central text in First Corinthians 11:3 cannot be saying that *every man* stands in the same relationship to *every woman* as Christ does to the man. That could not be true because if it is, then the woman is not in the Church. The great majority of the Protestant churches teach that individuals come to Christ through a personal confession of sins and a profession of faith in Jesus Christ as Lord and Savior. They teach that there is henceforth only one intermediary between God and the human race, the man Jesus Christ (see Romans 5:18, "Therefore as by the offence of one judgment came upon all men to condemnation; even so by the righteousness of one the free gift came upon all men [*anthropos*—human beings] unto justification of life").

Christ Is Head of His Church

The erroneous interpretation of First Corinthians 11:3 places every man squarely between the Redeemer and every woman. This is saying, in essence, "There is no salvation for women apart from the permission of every man." Unfortunately, it is possible to make the Bible say whatever you want to believe if you are willing to do so. No matter what you want to believe, you can find Scripture passages to misinterpret or remove from their proper settings to support your position or view—regardless of how outrageous it may be. The Holy Spirit isn't fooled, however, and neither are men and women who are filled with the Spirit of God.

A fellow came up to me recently after I stated that the man is not the spiritual head of the woman. "Oh yes he is!" he said. "The Bible says so. It says that as Christ is the head of the Church, so is the man the head of the woman [referring to Ephesians 5:23]." Then he asked me, "Is Christ the spiritual head of the Church?" I replied, "Yes." Thinking he had me locked into an irrefutable argument, he continued. "Then the man is the spiritual head of the wife." That is, he thought that until I asked him a question of my own, "...And Christ *is not* her spiritual head?" Without thinking, he said, "No, He isn't." Suddenly, he realized what he had just said and sputtered, "Oh yes, yes, she's in the Church." Then I said, "Well, if she's in the Church, and if she is a member of the Body of Christ, then Christ *is her head*, not the man."

The point I am making is this: Paul was simply illustrating that from the *family* or *domestic* standpoint, the man is the head of the wife *just as* from the *spiritual standpoint*, Christ is the head of the Church. He is not saying the husband is the wife's head spiritually. If that were true, then the born-again wife of an unsaved man would have no spiritual head! But, praise God, she does have a spiritual head...the Lord Jesus Christ Himself!

It is stupidity to maintain that a husband—any husband—has the right or ability to lord it over his wife's conscience and spirit! Jesus Christ alone is Lord over every wife and woman, just as much as He is the Lord over every husband and man.

Praise God, every human being can come to Christ *directly* without any mediator or priest—be they male, female, African-American, Japanese, Greek, Jewish, rich, or poor. Mary, the sister of Lazarus, was the "sinful" woman who dared to enter the house of Simon the Pharisee to anoint the feet of Jesus with precious oil of spikenard while she mixed her tears with the precious oil. She wiped the Master's feet with her hair and refused to bow to the disapproval of others. In fact, she braved the open disapproval of every man in that house to do what she did. She didn't care. She wasn't being rebellious; she was being desperate! She wanted the approval of only one man in that room—*Jesus Christ* (see Lk. 7:36-50; Jn. 11:2).

Great calamities might have been averted over the last 2,000 years of Church history if God's order in family government had been accepted and followed. Contrary to the misguided beliefs and teachings of some, God does not approve of husbands who "lord it over" their wives and children. Rather, husbands and wives are to be helpers together in all that concerns their temporal and eternal welfare.

It pleased God to ordain the husband to carry the greater responsibility for his family and those under his care. Therefore, He also vested him with greater authority in certain areas. If both husband and wife are what they should be, the husband will take his place naturally as the head of the family, and it will be joy to his wife to see him there. (No real woman wants a mere echo or a puppet for a husband.)

What About the Issue of "Submission"?

Submit to one another out of reverence for Christ. Wives, submit to your husbands as to the Lord. For the husband is the head of the wife as Christ is the head of the church, his body, of which he is the Savior. Now as the church submits to Christ, so also wives should submit to their husbands in everything. Husbands, love your wives, just as Christ loved the church and gave himself up for her (Ephesians 5:21-25 NIV).

Paul is talking to the whole Church when he says, "Submit to one another out of reverence for Christ" (Eph. 5:21). Does he mean we are to "lord it over" one another in the Church? No! It means we are to give in and fall into proper order, to be agreeable, and to get along with one another.

The word *submit* is translated from the Greek term *hupotasso*. It is translated as "submit" or "submitting" in the New International Version eight times in the New Testament. Of these eight occurrences, only two apply to the relationship of wives to their husbands in the home.[1]

The rest of the time, we are commanded to *hupotasso* or submit to leaders, to one another, to all authority, to God, and to our elders. In other words, this word *submit* is used for *all of us*, regardless of our gender. Paul uses this word twice to specifically describe the proper order and relationship of wife and husband in the *home*, and even in these instances, he specifically puts requirements and demands on the husbands that are even more stringent than those on the wives!

This same Greek term, *hupotasso*, appears a total of 41 more times and is translated as different words such as "subject," "subjection," "under obedience," "subdued," etc.[2] Again, most of these references have to do with *all of us* being obedient to those in authority.

What did the apostle Paul mean when he wrote, "Wives, submit yourselves unto your own husbands, as unto the Lord" (Eph. 5:22)? Does it mean the husband is to "lord it over" his wife? Does it mean that she is never to have any say so? No! It means that husbands and wives are to be agreeable and endeavor to get along with each other. The key to understanding this passage is *context*! If you take the time and trouble to read the verses before this passage and the verses that follow it, you will quickly realize that Paul is describing a situation where it would be *easy* to submit to someone.[3]

The controversial verse that says that "the head of the woman is the man," also says, "the head of Christ is God" (1 Cor. 11:3). Let me ask you this: Does this verse mean that Christ is essentially and eternally *inferior* to God the Father? If you replied "Yes," then how do you reconcile your view with Paul's statements proving Jesus' eternal equality with the Father?

> **Let this mind be in you**, *which was also in Christ Jesus: who,* **being in the form of God**, *thought it not robbery* **to be equal with God**: *but made Himself of no reputation, and took upon Him the form of a servant, and was made in the likeness of men: and being found in fashion as a man,* **He humbled Himself, and became obedient unto death**, *even the death of the cross. Wherefore God also hath highly exalted Him, and given Him a name which is above every name* (Philippians 2:5-9).

All of us are called to "take up our cross daily and follow Him" in the "death" of humility and obedience in this life (see Lk. 9:23-24). It is part of our life in Christ. We humble ourselves, and God exalts us. And this applies to *all of us* regardless of gender, color, rank, or social position. Jesus is our pioneer, our forerunner.[4] As our Savior and sacrifice, and as our very own Brother, He willingly took a *subordinate position* and was in all things obedient unto death. That allowed God the Father to highly exalt Him and place Him at His own right hand where Christ ever lives and makes intercession for us (see Heb. 7:25).

Likewise, when an individual, whether male or female, *submits* to the cross and receives Christ as Lord and Savior, that person is instantly transformed and raised to sit in the heavenlies with Christ according to the Book of Ephesians:

But God, who is rich in mercy, for His great love wherewith He loved us, even when we were dead in sins, hath quickened us together with Christ, (by grace ye are saved;) and hath raised us up together, and made us sit together in heavenly places in Christ Jesus (Ephesians 2:4-6).

Christ as God the Son is not "under" God the Father— yet He was under Him by choice and obedience to His Father during His earthly mission to take away the sins of the human race. When His mission was finished, God the Father raised up God the Son forever and seated Him at His right hand.

Now Jesus has raised us to "sit with Him" too. And we are told in Scripture:

For as many of you as have been baptized into Christ have put on Christ. There is neither Jew nor Greek, there is neither bond nor free, there is neither male nor female: for ye are all one in Christ Jesus (Galatians 3:27-28).

Now we are brought face to face with that which we have "feared." Our cherished ideas about submission and the inequality of the genders have been smashed and put in ruin. What do we do now? We turn to the Scriptures to put on the mind of Christ. This issue of "submission" is not a vertical matter, but a horizontal one. It has to do with function and order in the "life flow and work flow" of daily life, but it has *nothing* to do with individual worth or value in the sight of God. Jesus died for each of us and all of us, not just for a privileged or "more valued" few.

We all come to Him totally flawed, totally worthless in ourselves, and totally unable to redeem ourselves through our own religious accomplishments or supposed "worth." It takes the same measure of faith and supernatural power to redeem each of us and translate us out of darkness and into His marvelous light. Women are not some kind of "second cousin" redeemed unto God with a secondhand grace into a secondary place. As Paul told the Galatians, in Christ there is neither male nor female (see Gal. 3:28).

The Word of God says that we are "*joint*-[or co-]heirs with Christ" (Rom. 8:17). That means we are "shareholders," sharing in the grace of God as equals. Women are joint-heirs, as well as men. When Paul said, "For as many as are led by the Spirit of God, they are the *sons* of God" (Rom. 8:14), he used the Greek word *huios* for "sons." It means "offspring," and it is almost always used as a neutral term, implying both sons and daughters. W.E. Vine says it "primarily signifies the relation of *offspring* to parent (see Jn. 9:18-20; Gal. 4:30)."[5]

Jesus prayed, "That they *all* may be one; as Thou, Father, art in Me, and I in Thee, that they also may be one in Us..." (Jn. 17:21). That includes wives who are believers as well as husbands who are believers.

Much of what we have heard on this subject of submission cannot be substantiated by the Scriptures without purposely taking selected verses out of their contextual settings to make them say something that they don't really say. Sadly, this is exactly what has been done for hundreds of years to make women feel inferior to men to "keep them in their place." As a result, millions of women have felt compelled and pressured to take the place of a slave or servant. This kind of willful misrepresentation and interpretation of Scripture binds instead of loosens. This is in stark contrast to the declaration of Jesus Christ concerning the Word of God that "...ye shall know the truth, and the truth shall make you free" (Jn. 8:32).

Endnotes

1. James Strong, *Strong's Exhaustive Concordance of the Bible* (Peabody, MA: Hendrickson, n.d.), #G5293. The two references to wives submitting to husbands are Ephesians 5:22 and Colossians 3:18. All the following refer to other situations requiring submission: 1 Corinthians 16:16; Ephesians 5:21; Hebrews 13:17; James 4:7; 1 Peter 2:13; 5:5.

2. Strong's, #G5293.

3. We will look at this more closely in Chapter 7, "The Conclusion of the Matter."

4. Hebrews 12:2a in the Revised English Bible says, "Our eyes fixed on Jesus, the pioneer and perfecter of faith."

5. W.E. Vine, Merril F. Unger, William White, Jr., *Vine's Complete Expository Dictionary of Old and New Testament Words* (Nashville, TN: Thomas Nelson Publishers, 1989), 584.

Chapter 3

Must Wives **Always** Obey Their Husbands?

Women should remain silent in the churches. They are not allowed to speak, but must be in submission, as the Law says. If they want to inquire about something, they should ask their own husbands at home; for it is disgraceful for a woman to speak in the church (1 Corinthians 14:34-35 NIV).

But every woman that...prophesieth with her head uncovered dishonoureth her head... (1 Corinthians 11:5).

There is a reason that Paul seems to *forbid* in First Corinthians 14 what he seems to *allow* in chapter 11: women prophesying in the church. In the words of Bible commentator H.H. Halley, "There must have been some local circumstance, unbeknownst to us, that gave point to these instructions—possibly some bold women unbecomingly putting themselves forward."[1]

Cultural Context

First, we need to understand the "world of Paul" in A.D. 55, when it is believed that he wrote his first Epistle to the Corinthian church. Most of the early Christian congregations still met in local Jewish synagogues, or at the least, held on to most of the traditions of those meeting places.

Although Gentile women had no basis or background in the Old Testament Scriptures, Jewish women didn't have much more. They were generally excluded from the schools established in many synagogues to teach basic reading and writing skills to Jewish boys and to provide basic training in the Scriptures and in the law.[2] Instead, Jewish girls in Paul's day were "trained at home in household arts in preparation for marriage."[3]

The only access Jewish women had to the ancient Scriptures were the readings and sermons they heard every Sabbath in the synagogue and the Torah passages the entire family memorized as part of the feasts or standard worship rituals. When the Jews—and the Christian Jews—gathered for worship in their synagogues, the services would follow a common format and pattern, including the recitation of a creed, prayers, and readings from the law and the prophets (and later, from the Epistles and pastoral letters of the apostles).

Two things stand out as possible problem areas, causing Paul to say what he said in First Corinthians 14:[4]

1. The men were always seated separately from the women. In some synagogues, the women sat in elevated galleries well above the main floor where the men (and husbands) were

    seated. In other smaller structures, the women sat on one side of the room while the men sat on the other.

2. Traditional synagogue worship provided for a time after the sermon or homily for the men to *question* the one teaching from the Scriptures that day. This opportunity was not given to women in Paul's day, it being assumed that they had too little training in the Scriptures to ask appropriate questions, and that those questions were best asked of their husbands at home, where the wife would not have to shout across a large space and interrupt the entire congregation to get her husband's attention.

I've already noted that the Greek language has but one word for man, and none for husband; and only one word for woman, and none for wife. The only way to determine the specific meaning of these words is from the *context* in which they appear.

For instance, Paul is *not* talking about "all" women in his "no speaking" statement in First Corinthians 14. Why do I say this? Paul says in verse 35, "If they want to inquire about something, they should *ask their own husbands* at home..." (1 Cor. 14:35 NIV). The simple fact is that all women don't have husbands, so unmarried women are certainly not included in this text. Paul was dealing with a locally sensitive issue that was probably rooted in cultural customs unique to the Jewish culture, particularly in Corinth.

Context shows us that the Greek word *gyne* should have been rendered here as *wives*. "*Let your wives keep silence....*"

A.S. Worrell translates these verses, "Let your wives keep silence in the assemblies, for it is not permitted unto them to speak, but let them be in subjection as also saith the law. And if they wish to learn anything, let them ask their own husbands at home. For it is a shame for a wife to speak in an assembly."

It is also interesting to see that Paul the apostle refers us to "the law" when discussing women speaking in the church (see 1 Cor. 14:34). The word *law*, as used in the New Testament, refers to either the Ten Commandments, the five books of Moses called the Pentateuch, or the entire Old Testament.

Since the Ten Commandments say nothing about the rights of women, Paul must have been referring to the Pentateuch or the entire Old Testament. Why don't we see what the law says? Sometimes we suppose we know what the law says when we really don't. This is convenient because it allows us to interpret Scripture in the light of our own limited thinking rather than in the light of what God's Word actually says. It is also dangerous.

Creative Order?

Right from the beginning, we see in the Book of Genesis that God first made Adam and then Eve in a definite order, and then He gave *both* of them the power and right to subdue and have dominion over everything He made on the earth (see Gen. 1:26-28). Perhaps you have noticed that wild beasts have the same instinctive fear of women as they do of men, and that female animal trainers are just as effective as male animal trainers.

It is also important to understand that Eve was not taken from Adam's feet but from his side. Eve (and the female gender of the human race) was (and is) not created to be downtrodden, but to stand at the side of their male counterparts as co-heirs and full shareholders in all God's promises, gifts, and callings (see Gen. 2:21-22; 1 Pet. 3:1-7).

According to Genesis 2:18, God knew that it wasn't good for man to be without the help and inspiration of woman. So He made woman as a help meet and a helper worthy of him. Paul recognized that *interdependence* in his first letter to the Corinthians. (I want to quote from Weymouth's translation to clarify our understanding of the Greek text.)

> *Man does not originate from woman, but woman from man. For man was not created for woman's sake but woman for man's. ... Yet, in the Lord, woman is not independent of man nor man of woman. For just as woman originates from man, so also man has his birth through woman, but everything comes ultimately from God* (1 Corinthians 11:8-9,11-12 Weymouth).

There is no sign of inequality between man and woman in the Genesis account of creation. It was only after the "fall" that a curse (and prophetic blessing) was laid upon the wife. Isaac Leeser's translation from the original Hebrew makes this plain: "[In] Pain shall they bring forth children: and for thy husband shall be thy desire, but he shall rule over thee" (Gen. 3:16 Leeser). This was both penalty and prophecy, and it fell upon Eve, *not as a woman*, but *as a wife*.

Women are not subordinate to men, although they do have a subordinate place and function in God's order for the family unit. Even within that unit, they do not have a subordinate place in the Lord. The Bible says, "...there is neither male nor female: for ye are all one in Christ Jesus" (Gal. 3:28).

Women are called "sons of God" in the New Testament just as much as men are. John was writing to the entire Church (not just to men) when he said, "Beloved, now are we the sons [*teknon*] of God..." (1 Jn. 3:2). The Greek word *teknon* means "a child (as produced):—child, daughter, son."[5] That verse continues, "...and it doth not yet appear what we shall be: but we know that, when He shall appear, *we shall be like Him*; for we shall see Him as He is." Every woman who "sees" Him will be like Him just as much as the men who see Him. The power to be transformed doesn't come from our gender, our accomplishments, or our external physical attributes; it comes from *seeing Him as He is* when He appears.

God Sides With Who's Right

The "law" records several husband/wife teams and relationships as examples. Peter cited Sarah as a model wife whose worthy example Christian wives could follow: "Even as Sara obeyed Abraham, calling him lord: whose daughters ye are, as long as ye do well, and are not afraid with any amazement" (1 Pet. 3:6). I've heard many people try to lift this one verse out of the Bible and say, "See, the wife is to *obey the husband* just as Sarah obeyed Abraham." But does it mean that a wife doesn't have the right to speak her own mind? Some would leave the impression that the wife never has the right to express her thoughts, that she's under the rule and domination of her husband in all things. This reduces her to little more than a slave, and that isn't what Peter is saying. The "law" itself says:

*And Sarai said unto Abram, My wrong be upon thee: I have given my maid into thy bosom; and when she saw that she had conceived, I was despised in her eyes: the Lord judge between me and thee. But Abram said unto Sarai, Behold, thy maid is in thy hand; **do to her as it pleaseth thee***. *And when Sarai dealt hardly with her, she fled from her face* (Genesis 16:5-6).

In this passage, Abraham lets Sarah have her own way. He didn't dominate her like some warlord. This was the culmination of a disagreement described in chapters 16 through 21 of the Book of Genesis. In the end, God justified Sarah, not Abraham!

*Wherefore **she said unto Abraham, Cast out this bondwoman and her son***: *for the son of this bondwoman shall not be heir with my son, even with Isaac. And **the thing was very grievous in Abraham's sight** because of his son. And God said unto Abraham, Let it not be grievous in thy sight because of the lad, and because of thy bondwoman; **in all that Sarah hath said unto thee, hearken unto her voice***; *for in Isaac shall thy seed be called* (Genesis 21:10-12).

God told Abraham *to listen to his wife* in this situation. Sarah's counsel actually *overruled her husband's preferences* on this occasion, and God approved of it! Why? Because God always approves the right, regardless of who is right and who is wrong. The key is that Sarah kept a right attitude through it all, just like David maintained a pure heart in his dealings with another "authority" who was out of line (King Saul).

Some Spirit-filled ministers, I'm ashamed to say, have said to me that a woman has to do whatever her husband says "no matter what." Then they tell me that the Bible says a wife must obey her husband in all things. That is an insult to my intelligence and to God's righteousness! God will *never* side with wrong. That would be violating His very nature!

One fellow said to me, "If a husband asks his wife to drink with him, she ought to drink with him. If he wants her to go to the bar, she should go." (He told me these things personally.) You can understand that such thinking has created no little confusion. Another man said, "If an unsaved husband tells his wife not to go to church, *she's not to go.* If he tells her not to read the Bible, *she's not to read it.* She is to obey him to the letter."

Sarah was cited by the apostle Peter as a worthy example, and God sided with her and commanded her husband Abraham to "obey" his wife on one very important occasion. I'm sorry, but God is not going to side with any husband who thinks he can set aside God's Word and supplant God as the only being in the universe worthy of praise and absolute obedience. Such a man is deluded and in great danger. This kind of man reminds me of Nabal, an Old Testament husband who was literally named "Dolt" or "Fool." (He managed to live up to his name and die for it too!)

Abigail's Wisdom

Nabal's problems were rooted in his overbearing nature, and it put him in an early grave. Although David's men had protected Nabal's flocks, shepherds, and possessions for many years, when David's men asked for some food, Nabal angrily lashed out at them and sent them away. David and 200 armed and well-trained fighting men were already on their way to kill every male in Nabal's family that day when Nabal's wife, Abigail, found out about her husband's foolish stunt.

Abigail immediately arranged to personally intercept David with mules loaded down with food and drink. When they met, she took personal responsibility and asked David to forgive *her* for her husband's foolishness. His answer, and the fate of foolish Nabal, should sound a clear warning to "doltish" husbands everywhere:

*And David said to Abigail, Blessed be the Lord God of Israel, which sent thee this day to meet me: and blessed be thy advice, and blessed be thou, which hast kept me this day from coming to shed blood, and from avenging myself with mine own hand. For in very deed, as the Lord God of Israel liveth, which hath kept me back from hurting thee, except thou hadst hasted and come to meet me, surely there had not been left unto Nabal by the morning light any that pisseth against the wall. So David received of her hand that which she had brought him, and said unto her, Go up in peace to thine house; see, I have hearkened to thy voice, and have accepted thy person. And Abigail came to Nabal; and, behold, **he held a feast in his house, like the feast of a king**; and Nabal's heart was merry within him, for he was very drunken: wherefore she told him nothing, less or more, until the morning light. But it came to pass in the morning, when the wine was gone out of Nabal, and **his wife had told him these things, that his*** *heart died within him, and he became as a stone. And it came to pass about ten days after, that **the Lord smote Nabal**, that he died* (1 Samuel 25:32-38).

Abigail was a wise woman whose husband was a fool (and there are more cases like this out there too). The Bible called Nabal a "son of Belial." By disobeying her husband, Abigail saved a critical situation and won the favor of David. If she had listened to her husband, there would have been much bloodshed. Whether we like it or not, God blessed Abigail's actions, even though she "disobeyed" her husband.

Between Husband and Wife

Thank God for wives! They don't need to be put down; they need to be raised up in honor and treated with respect as partners in life, love, and godly destiny. Oh, I know there are some bossy wives out there who bring dishonor on their husbands, but if their husbands don't know how to take care of themselves, let them go ahead and be henpecked! You see, I believe that is *the husband's problem*. There's no use in downgrading all wives because of a few exceptions (and there's no use in downgrading all husbands because of a few overbearing and foolish exceptions either). It is the responsibility of the husband to take care of that—not the responsibility of the preachers.

If a man wants to be henpecked, it's his business and no one else's. I have no more business trying to manage another man's wife than I have managing his money! We can lay down principles, of course, but I think there are some men who rather enjoy being henpecked. If they do, let them enjoy it. Personally, I don't like being henpecked. I prefer to respect my wife, and I respect her opinion. I expect her to respect me and my opinion as well.

The first chapter of First Samuel tells us that when Hannah was still trying to wean little Samuel, she had a little difference with her husband, Elkanah, about accompanying him to offer the yearly sacrifice observed by all Jews. She spoke her mind and explained her reasons for wanting to stay home. Her way proved to be God's way, and Elkanah seemed to have no problem working with her:

> *But Hannah went not up; for she said unto her husband, **I will not go up** until the child be weaned, and **then I will bring him**, that he may appear before the Lord, and there abide for ever. And Elkanah her husband said unto her, **Do what seemeth thee good**; tarry until thou have weaned him; only the Lord establish His word...* (1 Samuel 1:22-23).

God's Commands Come First

It is not a sane argument to say that every wife must always obey her husband in everything. I want to repeat that statement: *It is not a sane argument to say that every wife must **always** obey her husband in everything.*

Some men are brutes who routinely require things of their wives that should not be granted or required of anyone! If an enraged husband commands his wife to kill their children, no sane person would say that she should obey. Yet the fact is that if a wife shouldn't obey that kind of command, then there are a lot of other things she shouldn't obey as well—because they are wrong! *A husband cannot countermand any of the Lord's commandments.*

I once heard someone tell the story of a man named Smith Wigglesworth, a great English evangelist and Pentecostal preacher, who spent most of his years as an unsaved plumber. He became so irritated by his wife's devotion to the things of God that he told her one day, "You go to church too much." Then he said, "I know enough about the Bible to know the man is the head of the wife. You're to obey me, and I say, 'Don't go to church!' So you're not to go."

Mrs. Wigglesworth smiled sweetly and said, "Now, honey, you are the head of this house, and you are my husband. Whatever you say in this house goes. And you know as well as I do that I do not neglect you, or the children, or the house in any way. *But you are not my Lord—Jesus is my Lord.*" She said, "The Bible tells us not to forsake the assembling of ourselves together. The Bible tells us to go to church, and I'm going."

"Well," Smith related, "I fumed and fussed and practically cussed." And finally one day he told her, "If you go tonight, I'll lock you out." She went to church anyway, and Smith locked her out of the house. She didn't have a key, so she couldn't get in when she returned that night. The next morning Smith Wigglesworth came downstairs and opened the back door. There she was, where she had huddled all night, bundled up in her coat with her back against the door. When Smith opened the door, she almost fell into the kitchen.

She could have really "let him have it" at that point, but instead Mrs. Wigglesworth bounded up with a smile and said, "Well, dear, how are you this morning?" She was so kind and sweet that her husband would have felt better if she had chewed him out. Instead, she just asked, "What would you like for breakfast, Smith?" She joyfully fixed her husband's favorite breakfast, and finally he couldn't take the guilt anymore. "All right, all right!" he said. "I'm wrong. I admit it!"

Mrs. Wigglesworth had just loved her husband back to God, but she did it at the same time that she stood her ground. If she had quit church and followed him, they both would have been in trouble. As a result, Smith Wigglesworth began to burn for Christ, and although he only began to minister in his 60's, he made a lasting impact for Jesus on several continents before he died at a ripe age, still ministering God's Word.

I remember one little woman in my ministry, who was always a particular inspiration to me. If I was trying to preach and both the sermon and the congregation were so dead that they needed a resurrection, all I had to do was look at this woman. She'd always inspire me to preach because her face was always lit up like a neon sign!

I'll never forget the time I looked down at her feet during a service and noticed that she was wearing galoshes! It hadn't rained in a month, so I just had to know why she was wearing those things. I found out that her husband didn't want her to go to church either (she was in good company with Mrs. Wigglesworth). He was so angry that he hid her shoes, figuring that if she couldn't find her only pair of shoes, then she wouldn't go to church.

That woman put on her galoshes and went anyway. I'm certain that if her husband had thrown away her galoshes, she would have gone barefoot! That precious saint was a meek little woman, but I remember her saying to me, "I don't want to dominate him in any way. He's my husband, and I respect him. He's the father of my children, and I teach them to respect him too. But he's not taking the place that he should take. He isn't interested in the things of God and won't come to church. It looks like I'm going to have to lead in these things. Am I wrong?"

"No," I told her, "you're not wrong. You're right." She stood her ground, and afterward she told me how she had told her husband: "Honey, I'm not trying to take any authority away from you, but I'm going to keep these children in Sunday school and in church. If they follow you, they'll be gambling and drinking. And, another thing, we ought to pray at the table. We just sit down and start eating like a bunch of hogs, so before we eat, I'm going to pray."

This woman didn't ask her husband if she could, she just said, "I'm going to do it." At the very next meal, she did just that. One of the children peeped and later told her, "Mama, Daddy just sat there and stared straight ahead like he was mad." It didn't stop her or slow her down. She just kept on praying before meals, and after a few times, he started bowing his head and closing his eyes along with the rest of them.

Then this woman said to her husband, "Honey, we ought to read the Bible in this home. It should be your place to do this, but you're not doing it. So before we retire every night, I'm going to read a chapter from the Bible and pray with the children. If you're here, you should have enough respect for me and the children to sit down and listen."

"Sometimes he would listen," she explained, "but at first, when I had the children get on their knees to pray, he'd just sit there. After awhile though, he would get off his chair and kneel too." Thank God this wife made her stand while still loving her man! As far as I know, every one of her children became a Christian, and her husband was saved later when he was nearly 60 years old!

You will never make it by compromising with the devil in any way! We need some balance in these things. A husband cannot countermand any of the Lord's commandments. He is the biblical "head of the home," but he is *not* the Lord over his wife's conscience. That place is reserved solely for the Lord Jesus Christ.

A wife must be true to her convictions, even at the cost of losing her husband, if necessary, when he will not endure her true devotion to Christ. We are to go to great lengths to save our marriages, but it isn't worth it to reject Christ for the sake of a spouse who rejects Him! Paul put it this way:

And the woman which hath an husband that believeth not, and if he be pleased to dwell with her, let her not leave him. For the unbelieving husband is sanctified by the wife, and the unbelieving wife is sanctified by the husband: else were your children unclean; but now are they holy. But if the unbelieving depart, let him depart. A brother or sister is not under bondage in such cases: but God hath called us to peace (1 Corinthians 7:13-15).

Endnotes

1. Henry H. Halley, *Halley's Bible Handbook* (Grand Rapids, MI: Zondervan Publishing House, 1973), 589.

2. Merrill C. Tenney, *New Testament Survey* (Grand Rapids, MI: Wm. B. Eerdmans Publishing Co., 1972), 99-100.

3. Tenney, *New Testament Survey*, 101.

4. *Eerdman's Handbook of the Bible* (Grand Rapids, MI: Wm. B. Eerdman's Publishing Company, 1973), 96.

5. James Strong, *Strong's Exhaustive Concordance of the Bible* (Peabody, MA: Hendrickson, n.d.), #G5043.

Chapter 4

Biblical Controversy and the Law of Interpretation

Let your women keep silence in the churches: for it is not permitted unto them to speak; but they are commanded to be under obedience, as also saith the law (1 Corinthians 14:34).

Let the woman learn in silence with all subjection. But I suffer not a woman to teach, nor to usurp authority over the man, but to be in silence. For Adam was first formed, then Eve (1 Timothy 2:11-12).

The two Scripture passages quoted here illustrate the type of statements that demand solid, time-proven exegesis and wise interpretation to bring understanding and appropriate application in our day. There is only one way to find the "mind of Christ" on issues that obviously change over time and culture. Although the Word of God, like God Himself, never changes but remains constant, God expects us to find balance and wisdom when applying the unchanging Word to our ever-changing environment and world. In other words, wisdom bids us "interpret the Word by the Word."

Remember these points covered in the previous chapters as we continue to examine the controversial issue of wives submitting to husbands: (1) Paul was not talking about *all* women in these controversial texts, but about wives in particular; and (2) he is talking about wives *learning something and asking questions during congregational meetings* (see 1 Cor. 14:35; 1 Tim. 2:11).

Proper translation and understanding of the original languages is very important. For instance, we have already learned that if you properly translate the Greek word *gyne* as "wife," rather than "woman," in the passages quoted above, these texts begin to make much more sense. In First Timothy, Paul is specifically referring to Adam and Eve in their roles as *husband and wife*; therefore, his injunction has to do with the "husband-wife proposition."

There is really no great danger of women in general "dictating to, domineering, or usurping authority" over men in general. It is far more likely and desirable that we will move closer to a true partnership in our various life roles. Some wives *have* been known to subject their husbands to such indignity in public, and these incidents produce some ungodly and unsettling fruit in society. What Paul is saying here is that wives are not to dictate to their husbands or usurp authority over them in their roles as head of the home and family.

We need to remember that women in Paul's day had little or no education because it simply wasn't considered necessary in ancient Middle Eastern cultures (it *still* isn't considered necessary among many Islamic and Hasidic

Jewish families today). Paul advised wives that if they wanted to learn more about a scriptural topic, then they should ask their husbands at home. This was directly related to the unacceptable alternative of these women raising their voices above that of the teacher or congregation to shout their question to a husband seated in an entirely different portion of the synagogue!

Paul's instruction also implied what was nearly always true in Paul's day: that the husband was better informed and educated than his wife due to the advantage of receiving a superior education. Few women could read or write in that day, and few were ever taught the Scriptures outside of what they heard in the weekly synagogue meetings and during holy sabbath celebrations. It was only natural and right that Paul direct inquiring women to consider their husbands as their first source of information concerning the Scriptures and points of theology.

It is a *fact* that this cultural reality from the first century isn't a reality in our Western culture today. If godly women were forced to depend on what their husbands told them about God, many would die in hopeless ignorance of the principles of our holy faith! All too many husbands can offer their families a sad collection of crude, half-baked, pernicious, and fallacious ideas about a God they do everything they can to avoid.

The Law of Scriptural Interpretation

There is one "law" that must govern our study and interpretation of God's Word: Every Scripture must be interpreted *in the light of what other Scriptures* say on the same subject. And any conclusion or declaration we make about a matter *must harmonize with all other Scripture.*

Much error has resulted from those who chose to ignore this law of interpretation. This kind of negligence and haphazard study and exegesis have produced most of the pain and difficulty we see concerning the role of "women" and countless other "controversial" subjects. The interpretation we put on our text Scriptures must harmonize with all other Scripture.

Most errors in exegesis and interpretation stem from one of at least three major areas of error:

1. Some people have lifted verses out of their contextual settings and have ignored the law of interpretation to purposely make the Scriptures say something in support of presupposed positions or ideas that the Scriptures have never condoned or supported.

2. Others have wandered off the path of truth because they did not interpret Scripture *in the light of other Scriptures*, despite the fact that they began with good motives and pure hearts. Many of our most grave errors in doctrine and belief were spawned by wonderful leaders who had beautiful spirits of love and were baptized with the Holy Ghost. Many such people were great witnesses and blessings to others—for awhile. But then they got off into error, leading many astray.

3. This last path of error is the path of shallow scholarship and halfhearted study and prayer over the Scriptures. Many ministers search the Scriptures solely to "scratch out a sermon" for a service, when God really wants them to dig

deeply into His riches to provide "fresh manna" for His people. As a result, they quickly grab the first "nugget" of truth they see and craft a sermon around it. Unfortunately, half-baked study and meditation produces half-baked food for the flock. This in turn produces half-baked theology and great "heartburn" in the poorly fed and often misled congregation!

One such man told me how God had brought him a great revelation. (Revelation is all right if it is in line with the Word. If it isn't—forget it.) I knew he was in trouble the moment he told me that he had a great revelation "which no one else knew about." Some of us have been in Pentecost a mighty long time, and we've seen certain things come up every now and then and fall. No one is exempt from Peter's solemn scriptural injunction:

Knowing this first, that no prophecy of the scripture is of any private interpretation. For the prophecy came not in old time by the will of man: but holy men of God spake as they were moved by the Holy Ghost. But there were false prophets also among the people, even as there shall be false teachers among you, who privily shall bring in damnable heresies, even denying the Lord that bought them, and bring upon themselves swift destruction. And many shall follow their pernicious ways; by reason of whom the way of truth shall be evil spoken of (2 Peter 1:20–2:2).

In my lifetime, I've seen some pretty ridiculous doctrines rise up to mislead many down the primrose path of heresy. I've seen the "God Is Dead" movement come and go in the modern era (although the oldest form of this dates from the day Jesus was crucified, and it fell apart on the third day when He arose from the dead). Another pernicious doctrine was the "revelation" that this fellow claimed he had received directly from God. He didn't realize that others before him had already fallen in to that particular pit, and they'd attached various pretty names to it such as "Eternal Restoration," "Ultimate Reconciliation," etc.

In essence, these people had failed (or refused) to take in "the whole counsel of God" when they decided that "everything" was going to be restored.[1] Basically, they taught that "everybody" will be saved! One group really took a leap off the diving board when they began to teach that even evil spirits (and possibly the devil himself) would be saved. All it took to "prove" their point, in their minds at least, was the few isolated Scripture verses they had carefully snipped out of their Bibles, which they felt supported their heretical position.

Another man who came to me with the *same revelation* was thrilled when he told me about the "new revelation" that he'd "found out from the Bible." It didn't take a lot of discernment on my part to smell out the problem. I could tell from his breath he'd been drinking, and during our conversation he would curse and use God's name in vain from time to time for emphasis.

This man was ecstatically happy, and he laughed as he told me, "Our preacher preached—and I've found out from the Bible it is true—that *everybody's going to be saved*. It doesn't make any difference what you do. Isn't it wonderful! You know, *the Bible says* that with God all things are possible. And *the Bible says* that God's not willing that any should perish...." Then he wanted to make sure I was with him, so he asked me, "Are all things possible to God?"

"Yes," I answered.

"Is God all-powerful? all-knowing? all-wise?" he asked.

"Yes."

"Well, He's plainly said He's not willing that any should perish," the man said, gathering momentum for his big finale. "So *nobody's going to perish*. Everybody will be saved! I've been so thrilled since I found that out." I made sure this misguided man knew exactly where I stood before we parted, and I made sure he knew where God stood too.

I remember a Full Gospel minister who for many years had demonstrated a real ministry in getting people saved and baptized in the Holy Ghost—until he got off into the *same error*! "For years," he said, "I thought my alcoholic uncle, who died cursing God, went to hell. But now I've found out that he went to Heaven. He's saved because God's not willing that any should perish, and God's all-powerful. I used to talk to him years ago about accepting Christ, but he'd curse me and send me on my way. He never did make a profession of Christ. But I know now he went straight through to the glory world."

Have you noticed a pattern emerging here? Each of the people in the examples I've given basically quoted Scripture verses correctly. It is true that "with God all things are possible" (see Mt. 19:26; Mk. 10:27). It is also true that the apostle Peter told us, "God is not willing that any should perish..." (see 2 Pet. 3:9). Yes, they are correct when they say God can do anything. They are also correct when they say God is all-powerful. The problem is that they didn't harmonize these Scriptures with other Scriptures.

In this particular example, these people broke the "law of interpretation" by failing to compare their "revelation" with the clear teachings of the Lord Jesus Christ. Jesus taught that some folks would be lost. He said, "...Go ye into all the world, and preach the gospel to every creature. He that believeth and is baptized shall be saved; *but he that believeth not shall be damned*" (Mk. 16:15-16).

Had they heeded the whole counsel of God, they would have quickly realized that they were in the grips of an extreme doctrine. The doctrine of "ultimate reconciliation" in reality is erroneous, devilish, misleading, and damaging to the Body of Christ.

Now coming back to this "woman question," can you see some similar errors in the way some preachers have failed to measure their "revelation" of the subjugation of women against the testimony of God's full counsel?

Are We Consistent in Our Interpretation?

When one man tried to make a "women should submit" point with a verse of Scripture that he was clinging to, I pointed out to him another Scripture. "Well," he said, "there may have been some exceptions. But this is the way God wants it." No! If an interpretation doesn't harmonize with all other Scriptures, then the interpretation is wrong. One of the most significant Scripture passages contradicting (and confounding) many people who cling to the "extreme submission" position for all women is found in the Book of Joel and is recorded for us again in the Book of Acts:

*For these are not drunken, as ye suppose, seeing it is but the third hour of the day. But this is that which was spoken by the prophet Joel; And it shall come to pass in the last days, saith God, I will pour out of My Spirit upon **all flesh**: and your sons **and your daughters shall prophesy**, and your young men shall see visions, and your old men shall dream dreams: and on My servants **and on My handmaidens** I will pour out in those days of My Spirit; and **they shall prophesy*** (Acts 2:15–18).

Hundreds of years before the day of Pentecost, the prophet Joel prophesied, "And it shall come to pass afterward, that I will pour out My spirit upon *all* flesh..." (Joel 2:28). As Peter said on the day of Pentecost, "This is the fulfillment of Joel's prophecy."

We still live in that dispensation today—the Holy Ghost dispensation. God has poured out of His Spirit upon *all* flesh, and that includes women as well as men. The prophet made it impossible to "revise" his words when he specifically said, "...and your sons *and your daughters* shall prophesy...."[2]

When I first encountered "Full Gospel people," I had fellowship with them primarily because of my interest in divine healing. I just "closed my ears" to the other things that they taught. But I knew they had revelation on divine healing that I hadn't seen in any other churches. I'd been healed by the power of God, and I had been standing in faith alone. So when I found these folks it strengthened my faith to fellowship with them. Even though I was of another denomination, I would attend every Full Gospel service I could get to.

Some of my friends warned me about "those Pentecostal people" when I was a young man many years ago. One man in particular was a seminary graduate whom I'd known all my life. He told me one night after we had discussed the "Pentecostal thing" for hours, "Now, Clarence, you ought to be careful about going around those Full Gospel people. I'll admit they're good people. And I'll admit they live stricter and straighter lives than most folks in our own church do. But..." he warned, "that speaking with tongues is of the devil."

"Is it?"

"Yes, it is."

"Well now," I said, "it seems a little strange to me that people could have something from the devil that would help them live better lives than we do. The way I'm able to ascertain it, the works of the devil make people worse—not better." (I didn't see speaking with tongues as positively then as I do now, but oddly enough, instead of hindering me, my friend's objections helped me to see that it must be good!)

"Those Pentecostal people," he went on to say, "have got to be wrong."

"Why?" I asked.

"They've even got *women preachers*!"

"They do?"

"Yes. They let women teach, testify, and take a prominent place—right in the very church service. And that is wrong."

"Is it?"

"Yes, it's wrong for women to preach, or take the lead in any way. The Bible says, 'Let your women keep silence in the church....'"

"Our women don't."

"Oh, well," he said, "we let them teach over in the Sunday school building, but not in the church."

"That's ridiculous!" I said. "And it is exactly what Jesus said the Jews were doing when He cleansed the temple. They'd say, 'Oh, the temple is holy right around the altar, but the rest of it isn't holy. You can do what you want to in the other areas. You can sell sheep and cheat people out there.' But Jesus took a whip and drove out the money changers.

"That Sunday school annex," I went on, "is just as holy as the sanctuary. And besides that, as far as having church is concerned, it's where two or three are gathered that people are having church. It's not the building. The building is just a place to meet."

Under the new covenant, church is not confined to any building. Paul wrote several times, as did others, about the church "in so-and-so's house." You can have church in the open air, a barn loft, downtown in a little mission, in a tent, or in a great cathedral.

Now, I knew this Bible teacher thought that to "prophesy" meant to preach. And there is an element of truth in that, but not all prophesying is preaching, and all preaching is not prophesying. But I knew he thought that when the Bible spoke of prophesying, it meant preaching exclusively (anything else would move him uncomfortably close to that "Pentecostal stuff"). So I said, "Peter quoted Joel's prophecy on the day of Pentecost. So we have both an Old Testament and a New Testament witness telling us that under this dispensation *the daughters will prophesy as well as the sons*. To prophesy means to preach, doesn't it? [I was going to play along with him to make a key point.] *Is it wrong for them to preach?*" That one got him.

"Uh-h-h-h. Uh-h-h-h. I'll have to give that a little more thought," he said.

"While we're on the subject," I said, "let me say something else. We send women into the mission fields, and these female missionaries teach and preach on foreign fields. They don't just teach children either; they teach other women and men as well. One of our own mission magazines recently told about a mission station *where there is no man*. A lady is heading it up. That means that she is really heading up what you would call a local church, and we've put our stamp of approval on it.

"I believe it's inconsistent to say to them, 'Ladies, you can't talk over here. You can't speak in the main assembly, and we won't ordain you. [Some have since been ordained in this particular denomination. This conversation with my friend took place 40 years ago.] You have to be quiet. But we will recognize the call of God on your life, so we'll send you to the mission field. You can't teach or preach to men over here, but you can over there.' Then we send them to the front lines, where it's the hardest. What's the difference," I asked him, "between preaching to the heathen over there and preaching to the heathen here?" (He had no answer because there wasn't one.)

We must base our thoughts, actions, and beliefs on the Word of God. And when things don't seem clear to us, we need to interpret the Word *by the Word*. If a thing still isn't clear to us, then we have no business formulating doctrines, dogmas, or opinions about them until God brings clarity on the subject (that is in alignment with the "whole counsel of God").

Endnotes

1. The New King James Version quotes the apostle Paul as saying, "For I have not shunned to declare to you *the whole counsel of God*" (Acts 20:27). Paul was saying that he preached it all, not just the "pleasing" parts of the gospel message. He preached the blood, repentance from sins, the truth of the cross, and the glory of the resurrection. He preached about both Heaven *and* hell to make sure people knew the destinations determined by their choices. We need to do the same, comparing the Scriptures to the full body of Scripture for proper context and godly application.

2. Acts 2:17; Joel 2:28-29.

Chapter 5

Covered Heads, Social Customs, and "Naturalness"

Early in the history of the Church, the leaders in Jerusalem were confronted with a potentially divisive problem that demanded a very unconventional solution. Much to their shock, Peter the Jewish apostle first, and then Paul the Pharisee turned apostle, reported to the predominantly Jewish leaders of the first church congregation in history that *Gentiles, non-Jewish believers*, had been baptized in the Holy Ghost just like the Jews in Jerusalem![1]

What were they to do with them? At that point, Christianity was still considered a branch, or "cult," of Judaism, and the apostles still preached the gospel to large crowds in the temple of Herod at times. The law required that all new converts to Judaism (and, therefore in their minds, to Christ) be circumcised and come under all the restraints of the law.

New Testament Precedent

In the end, after heated discussion and testimony, James the apostle declared the decision to set aside as non-binding the Jewish requirements of circumcision and adherence to the Levitical diet restrictions and sabbaths that devout Jews had followed for thousands of years![2] How could they do such a thing? They realized that the ancient prophets, the law, the teachings of Jesus Christ, and recent divine revelation demonstrated that what was appropriate before Christ was no longer needed after the cross. They also knew that what was required in the Jewish culture was not necessarily required in non-Jewish settings.

This same problem of discerning the will of God for the present-day generation is still with us. Many Christians have been confronted with this problem over the years when they turn to certain passages in Paul's writings in the Book of First Corinthians:

> *But I would have you know, that the head of every man is Christ; and the head of the woman is the man; and the head of Christ is God.* ***Every man praying or prophesying, having his head covered, dishonoureth his head.*** *But every woman that prayeth or prophesieth with her head uncovered dishonoureth her head: for that is even all one as if she were shaven. For if the woman be not covered, let her also be shorn: but if it be a shame for a woman to be shorn or shaven, let her be covered. For a man indeed ought not to cover his head, forasmuch as he is the image and glory of God: but the woman is the glory of the man. For the man is not of the woman; but the woman of the man. Neither was the man created for the woman; but the woman*

for the man. For this cause ought the woman to have power on her head because of the angels. Nevertheless neither is the man without the woman, neither the woman without the man, in the Lord. For as the woman is of the man, even so is the man also by the woman; but all things of God. Judge in yourselves: is it comely that a woman pray unto God uncovered? Doth not even nature itself teach you, that, if a man have long hair, it is a shame unto him? But if a woman have long hair, it is a glory to her: for her hair is given her for a covering. But if any man seem to be contentious, we have no such custom, neither the churches of God (1 Corinthians 11:3-16).

A hasty reading of this great text might lead you to believe that Paul laid upon all women everywhere—and for all time—the command to wear a veil or to keep their heads covered in church services. Many conscientious women today are afraid to remove their hats or "coverings" in church services lest they violate this passage.

The crux of the matter hinges on this question: *Is this specific instruction by Paul binding everywhere and for all times?* Let's examine this Scripture carefully then, for if it binds us now, we should obey it.

Upon what does Paul base his argument for women covering their heads in a religious service? First, he does *not* say it is irreverent. Nor does he say it is displeasing to God. If he had, there would be no questions about this command.

Deference to Head

Earlier we discussed what Paul said about husbands being the "head" of their wives. This is the basis of Paul's argument.

Now I want you to realize that the head of every man is Christ, and the head of the woman is man, and the head of Christ is God. Every man who prays or prophesies with his head covered dishonors his head. And every woman who prays or prophesies with her head uncovered dishonors her head—it is just as though her head were shaved. If a woman does not cover her head, she should have her hair cut off; and if it is a disgrace for a woman to have her hair cut or shaved off, she should cover her head. A man ought not to cover his head, since he is the image and glory of God; but the woman is the glory of man (1 Corinthians 11:3-7 NIV).

In our country, we instinctively (or culturally) sense the impropriety of men covering their heads in religious services. I've been in many services in which a man would come in and sit down with his hat still on, and one of the ushers would go to him and ask him to remove it.

Among modern Jews, however, the opposite custom prevails. In Orthodox Jewish synagogues today, men are *required* to keep their heads covered. If a man comes to a service without the customary covering, one is provided for him.

When we visited the Muslim temple in Jerusalem, we pulled off our shoes and left them at the door. In Muslim countries, the worshipers remove, not their hats, but their shoes. Perhaps this dates from the time the Lord said to Moses, "...put off thy shoes from off thy feet, for the place whereon thou standest is holy ground" in Exodus 3:5 (the Muslims regard Moses as one of their prophets too).

According to the Bible record, nothing was said to Moses about his head gear on that occasion.

Why then does Paul protest against men praying or prophesying with their heads covered? This will be made clearer later, but suffice it to say here that the veil, or covering, was an acknowledgment that someone present (though possibly not visible) was his "head" or covering authority.

In the same passage, Paul said a woman who prayed or prophesied with her head uncovered dishonored "her head." He didn't say she dishonored God, *but her head*. I believe this was a reference to her husband who was present in the same meeting.

The veil was (and is in many Middle Eastern cultures) a symbol of subjection to her husband, much as a wedding band is a public symbol of belonging and covenant commitment. So thoroughly was it recognized as a badge setting forth the wife's private and subordinate position that it continues even in Christian traditions and ceremonies as the significant rite of "assuming the veil" in nearly all marriage ceremonies. The custom of "taking the veil" still lingers in the Roman Catholic ceremonies for those becoming nuns, or "brides of Heaven," in a marriage of Christ. Laying aside the veil, then, by Christian women, meant that as a member of the Body of Christ they no longer were in a subordinate position.

The Greek word *exousia* is translated as "power" in Paul's discourse on "coverings": "For this cause ought the woman to have power on her head because of the angels" (1 Cor. 11:10). It is also translated variously as *authority, liberty*, and in the plural as *authorities* and *potentates*.[3]

An "informed" paraphrase of this verse that sounds so strange to our ears would read like this:

"For this reason [because of the facts stated in verses 8 and 9] ought the wife to have a sign of her husband's authority, a covering on her head, because of the angels."

Here again, it is not a "woman question," but a "husband-wife question." Out of deference or honor for Christ, Paul said a man (or husband) should *not* cover his head. Out of honor for her husband (and also out of deference for the angels who were recognized as present at public worship, and who would be grieved with any disorder), the apostle said a wife *should* cover her head. Was he "majoring on the minors," or was he struggling to give a culturally appropriate outward symbol to demonstrate an eternal spiritual principle of submission to proper authority? I think the latter is true.

In Bible times, believers had far more regard for the presence and ministry of angels than we see today. Frankly, I think it might have a wholesome effect on our assemblies and prayer groups if we were more aware and respectful of the presence of these heavenly messengers among us. The fact is, they *are* present because the Word of God says so.[4]

In one particular church covenant the following expression is found: "We do now in the presence of God, angels, and this assembly most solemnly and joyfully enter into this covenant...." It is interesting to me that such an important document would so prominently recognize the presence of angels.

Deference to Social Custom

Another reason Paul offers to support his recommendation that women cover their heads in church services is "social custom." Paul's statement about "custom" to the Corinthians is translated this way by the New Living Translation of the Bible: "But if anyone wants to argue about this, all I can say is that we have no other custom than this, and all the churches of God feel the same way about it" (1 Cor. 11:16).

Paul said earlier in his letter, "...but if it be a shame for a woman to be shorn or shaven, let her be covered" (1 Cor. 11:6). Paul was saying that if a married woman appeared in a public church service without her head covered, it would amount to the same thing as appearing with her hair cut, or her head shaved. And *that practice* was contrary to the prevailing custom in Corinth. In Greece it was the custom for women to cover their heads with a corner of their shawls when they were in a public area. They did not need to cover their heads when in a place shielded from the public eye.

This is generally not customary in modern Western society. A woman does not appear to be more modest if she wears a veil or hood on her head in public. True womanly modesty is recognized now as much by the frank unassuming manner, the open countenance, and the sincere look of her eyes as it was in the days of Paul in Corinth by the wearing of the veil.

Virtuous married women proudly wore coverings on their heads as open badges of willing subjection to (and covenental oneness and attachment to the name of) their husbands. A married woman appearing in the church with her head uncovered in Paul's time in Corinth would have scandalized the church. Strangers would have thought such a woman was an immoral woman of the city "offering her wares" to the willing. Such conduct would reflect poorly on her *and on her husband*. It would have amounted to willful and open rebellion and rejection of her marriage vows to her husband, bringing stinging dishonor to her head, her husband.

We have our own versions of social laws and customs too. At the turn of the century—right here in America—it was a custom in most churches for the men to sit on one side and the women on the other. I've been in the ministry for 40 years, and a number of years ago I preached in churches where this custom still prevailed. A woman didn't dare sit on the men's side because it was against their custom. And a person needed to abide by it, or else the congregation would think that he or she was out of line.

An Appeal to Naturalness

Paul makes one more appeal to our sense of "naturalness" when he said, "Doth not even nature itself teach you, that, if a man have long hair, it is a shame unto him? But if a woman have long hair, it is a glory to her..." (1 Cor. 11:14-15).

Notice again that Paul *didn't say God said it*. He said, "Does not even *nature*...." He goes to nature to prove a point. In the 2,000 or so years that have passed since that time, small wars have been fought and countless churches have been disrupted over the question, "Does the Bible teach that women should have long hair?"

How long is long? And how short is short? I have had the experience of pastoring various churches over several years. Somehow I got by in certain places, even though my wife didn't have long hair like the other ladies did. Invariably, these ladies would take their long hair and twist it up tightly on their heads in a knot.

Paul appealed to "naturalness," but I believe he knew our ideas of "naturalness" change from era to era and from culture to culture. However, in general, it is true that when a woman's hair is longer than the way men ordinarily wear their hair, then you can easily tell she is a woman—even from a distance. We know from paintings and illustrations of certain periods in history that men wore their hair longer than we ordinarily do today, but at the same time women wore theirs a little longer than that. Even in those eras, men wore their hair shorter than women according to the standards of the day.

Let me say this before we go any further: I don't think it is good for any Christian man or boy to be the least bit "effeminate," because the Word of God clearly speaks against it. We need to honor the Word of God on every occasion. The wise man in Ecclesiastes said, "Let us hear the conclusion of the whole matter: Fear God, and keep His commandments: for this is the whole duty of man" (Eccles. 12:13).

So let's sum up Paul's points:

1. He does not say it is irreverent for women to appear with their heads uncovered. He doesn't even insinuate it.

2. He does not say it displeases God.

3. He does say it is the custom and that it is wise to abide by the custom.

4. He appeals to naturalness.

Paul dealt with broad principles of *universal application*. But as times and customs have altered in regard to feminine proprieties, I see nothing in this passage to prevent women from appearing in public with their heads uncovered in the United States. In our culture, it is far more important to make sure that you are "under authority" when you gather to worship the King of kings than to wear some outer sign of something that is actually missing from your inner man!

Jesus and those who followed in His footsteps always went straight for the heart, because the outward things meant nothing if the heart was wrong. If you find yourself in another place or culture where it is the custom to cover your head, then I would encourage you to abide by it so you will not be an offense or bring an offense to another.

Endnotes

1. Acts 10:44–11:18, the first occurrence with Peter.

2. Acts 15:1-31, the second and final occurrence with Paul and Barnabas.

3. James Strong, *Strong's Exhaustive Concordance of the Bible* (Peabody, MA: Hendrickson, n.d.), #G1849.

4. Mt. 18:10; Lk. 2:9-15; Jn. 20:12; Heb. 1:13-14; 13:2.

Chapter 6

Proper Dress, Adornment, and "Pantsuits"

*In like manner also, **that women adorn themselves** in modest apparel, with shamefacedness and sobriety; not with broided hair, or gold, or pearls, or costly array; but (which becometh women professing godliness) **with good works** (1 Timothy 2:9-10).*

*Likewise, ye wives, be in subjection to your own husbands; that, if any obey not the word, **they also may without the word be won by the conversation of the wives;** while they behold your chaste conversation coupled with fear. **Whose adorning** let it not be that outward adorning of plaiting the hair, and of wearing of gold, or of putting on of apparel; **but let it be the hidden man of the heart**, in that which is not corruptible, even the ornament of a meek and quiet spirit, **which is in the sight of God of great price.** For after this manner in the old time the holy women also, who trusted in God, **adorned themselves**, being in subjection unto their own husbands (1 Peter 3:1-5).*

You and I should be quick to acknowledge that our Lord Jesus Christ has authority over us. Yet we must also understand and accept the fact that because He is our Lord, He also has the authority to regulate our apparel and everything else pertaining to us.

At the beginning of this chapter, I quoted the two most-quoted Scripture passages dealing with outward apparel and Christian women. These Scriptures deal with a temptation that—even though men are not immune to it—nevertheless usually makes its strongest appeal to women. For this reason, I believe, women are singled out by Paul and Peter for this especially strong and direct counsel.

In our day we have seen that fashion often exerts a greater power over many women than does any sense of godly modesty. Even worldly men have been shocked by the scantiness of the clothing worn by many women professing to be Christians. It is to be deplored that so many Christian women adopt fashions designed for and by people of questionable character, rather than by those who seek to live for the glory of God. By their actions, these women seem to indicate they are more interested in arousing the sexual hormones of men in the Church than in pleasing God and bringing all glory to His holy name! Who would want to stand before the Almighty Judge to answer for that particular charge?!

In any case, I do not see that either Paul or Peter were laying down *strict and ironclad rules that were to be universally applied in every culture and every era that would follow them.* However, I do believe there is an eternal and unchanging principle involved that does indeed apply in every culture and every generation.

I can hear the voices raised in protest even now: "But Peter told women not to plait their hair or wear gold!" According to my research, it was the custom of the Gentile culture in Corinth for women to spend much time plaiting the hair and working gold and other precious trinkets into their complex hair braids. It was this excessive placement of personal identity, worth, and the practice (which we follow today) of openly parading wealth and physical attractiveness as a sign of personal value that Paul and Peter were addressing.

While the critics quote these famous passages and conclude, "Paul and Peter told women not to fix their hair," I teach women to dress up and look nice for themselves and for their husbands! I warn them, "You had to look nice to get him, and you'd better look nice if you want to *keep* him." Frankly, no one is honored or blessed if God's ladies go out of their way to look poor, downtrodden, joyless, and unattractive. The fact is, the apostles weren't asking women to do so.

Don't Put on Clothes?

Peter wasn't saying "don't" in his epistle. If he actually said "*don't* plait your hair" and "*don't* wear gold," then it is clear by the grammatical construction of his entire statement that he was also saying in ironclad terms, "*don't put on clothes*"! Look at his statement again: "Whose adorning let it not be that outward adorning of plaiting the hair, and of wearing of gold, or of putting on of apparel" (1 Pet. 3:3). Of course, we know that Peter did not tell Christian wives "not to wear apparel"!

The apostle was dealing with the especially strong temptation to women in this area of outward adornment. By

God's design, men are especially attracted to the outward appearance of women, and a husband is often judged directly according to his wife's physical appearance and outward demeanor. Peter was saying, "Don't put so much emphasis on and spend all your time on dresses and clothes. Don't devote all your time and energy on fixing up. Don't spend all your time on dresses and clothes." (If some Christian women spent half as much time praying, fasting, and seeking God as they do on their hair and clothes, *they'd be spiritual giants*!) Peter is trying to strike a balance here.

We need balance. The Church has a tendency to get into a ditch on one side of the road or the other, but we don't need to go to extremes either way. We need to go down the middle of this road.

Peter's point is simply this: *Don't spend all your time on the outward man*. See to it, first of all, that the inward man is adorned with a meek and quiet spirit. If you will tend to the man on the inside first, you won't have to worry so much about the fellow on the outside.

When I received the Holy Ghost, churches were a little more strict in the areas of clothing, outward appearance, makeup, and jewelry than they are now. Almost all the women in fundamental evangelical and Pentecostal churches had long hair because they were taught to do so.

Bobbed Hair and Conniption Fits

I remember the time one lady caused an uproar when she cut her hair, or "bobbed" it, as they called it. Some may not understand my terminology, but natives of Texas and Oklahoma will get the picture when I say the people "threw conniption fits"!

This particular woman minister responded by saying, "God told me to do it." When her accusers answered with their fingers thumping their open Bibles, "But the Bible says right here, 'for a woman to have long hair'!" Her answer is worth repeating here:

> "You see, though, there are other Scriptures [remember that the Scriptures must be interpreted in the light of other Scriptures] that tell me otherwise. I saw that Peter said, 'Don't spend all your time on your outward man—on your hair—but see to it, first of all, that the inward man is adorned with a quiet and meek spirit.' *It dawned on me that I was spending too much time on my long hair, trying to look nice.* Since I've cut my hair, I just run a comb through it, and I'm finished. I can spend my time with my Bible and praying. Really, I'm more spiritual and have a closer walk with God now than before. I was spending too much time with the outward man."

There is a balance to be struck here. I would counsel women who preach the gospel to be especially careful to avoid even the "appearance of evil" or immodesty (see 1 Thess. 5:22). It might be wise for those women who take some place of leadership to lean more toward the conservative side on issues such as this.

Paul counsels women, in lieu of going to excess about these things, to have, or "to be adorned," with good works. You can readily see that if a woman spends too much time in some of these areas, she wouldn't have time for good works. Even worse, she will begin to attach a good part of her identity and affections to these outward things. Peter counsels us to look to the adorning of the "inward man" instead. It takes time to adorn the inward man. Frankly, it comes down to the age-old battle within all of us between the flesh and the spirit.

I don't think we need to lay down ironclad rules and a list of outward "do's and don'ts." Nor do we have the right to force our opinions and ideas on others.

I was always very conservative. It took years before I began to wear a ring because it was commonly frowned upon among the people I'd associated with for years. But I didn't have any convictions about others wearing them—it wasn't any of my business. I'm not to regulate your conscience; you are. That's between you and God. Let every man work out his own salvation (see Phil. 2:12).

How About Nose Rings, Lord?

I never did care for the earrings ladies wear, but that wasn't any of my business. In my own relationship with my wife, I wasn't mean about it, but I just expressed my desire in as loving a way as I could, and my wife didn't wear earrings. Finally, I told her to do what she wanted to do and wear them if she wanted. I didn't see that God particularly cared. After all, I saw that God saved people in Africa and gloriously baptized them with the Holy Ghost—even while they were wearing rings in their noses! (It sounds like a transcontinental "replay" of the Jewish/Gentile controversy in Acts, doesn't it?)

Is It True That a Woman Cannot Wear Pantsuits?

I can't tell you how many times I've been asked this question or have heard it voiced over the last 20 or 30 years, but my answer has always been the same: "No, this is not true for a strict interpretation of the Word. Pray about it. Let the Lord guide you in this." Here is what the Scriptures say about this problem in general:

> *The woman shall not wear that which pertaineth unto a man, neither shall a man put on a woman's garment: for all that do so are abomination unto the Lord thy God* (Deuteronomy 22:5).

The Scriptures warn godly women to avoid dressing in ways that are distinctly masculine, and likewise they warn men to abstain from wearing women's clothing or taking on feminine appearances in any way.

In our modern society, we are well aware of the fact that some homosexuals like to wear women's clothes or even alter their physical bodies to look like women or impersonate women. It is my opinion that *this* was the problem that the patriarchs were addressing in the Old Testament, not the simple act of wearing clothes that were sometimes worn by members of the opposite sex. One thing is certain: a woman should strive to be a woman whether she is wearing slacks or a dress.

Ever Seen a Man in a Pantsuit?

Older church tradition in North America used to say that women should not wear pants, because pants were supposedly reserved for men, while skirts and dresses were reserved for women. The Bible says nothing to this effect, and actual practice has varied from region to region in the United States. (By the way, women's "pantsuits" are not men's clothing. I don't know of a single man who would want to be seen wearing a woman's "pantsuit" outfit!)

In some areas of the extreme north where frigid temperatures, inclement weather, and high winds are common much of the year, dresses were absolutely inappropriate wear for those women who wanted to survive. The same was true in some ranching areas of the western states where women worked as hard as men did, spending much of their time on horseback working with the stock.

Once again, I counsel women to let grace and consideration for others guide them. If you are a woman called to minister to a group of people who have another view concerning appropriate apparel for women, then you need to conform to their standards lest you be a stumbling block to them. If you feel that you cannot conform, then you should pray about moving on to work with another group that shares your convictions.

I find it interesting that throughout all the arguments and debates I've heard over the years, very few people have brought up the obvious fact that our Savior Himself and all the men of His era wore "dresses," or outer tunics, along with a "girdle," or wrap, around the waist. If we want to be literalists, there may be some very embarrassed "hard-liner" preachers in our churches walking around in full-length dresses. We need to be very careful about laying down hard-and-fast rules and regulations concerning clothing and appearance.

It is very important that each of us follow peace in our decisions and actions (see Heb. 12:14; Col. 3:15). Some of us have a strong background of teaching against women wearing pants. Wear what your society or fellowship of believers permits you to wear, but do not try to force your views in a dictatorial way on someone else. You can share your convictions, but do not demand.

Whose adorning let it not be that outward adorning or plaiting the hair, and of wearing of gold, or of putting on of apparel; but let it be the hidden man of the heart...even the ornament of a meek and quiet spirit, which is in the sight of God of great price (1 Peter 3:3-4).

Here, women are admonished to put the emphasis of their lives on "the hidden man of the heart" because this is the emphasis of God! They are to be tender and feminine with a gentle and quiet spirit. We need to focus on humility of spirit rather than on our outward dress and appearance. People are far more impressed with inward beauty than with mere outward attractiveness. I know that in my experience, some of the so-called "holy" women who paraded around in their "righteousness of the clothesline" were some of the meanest women in the world! Any possible sense of holiness they possessed was literally overpowered by the "holier-than-thou" spirit they had developed. We need to remember that our most powerful weapon for Christ is *love*, not our wardrobe or lack of cosmetics. It is love alone that covers a multitude of sins (see 1 Pet. 4:8).

Chapter 7

The Conclusion of the Matter

Missionaries tell us that in the Eastern countries—especially prior to World War II—the poor, illiterate women often were not able to comprehend the meaning of the gospel message. As a result, they would frequently interrupt the service with foolish and irreverent questions.[1] For instance, they would abruptly speak out in meetings and interrupt sermons or teachings just to ask about the cost of the missionary's dress, or the purpose of some article of attire!

It is very possible that this is an accurate picture of the situation Paul was dealing with when he stated his restrictions concerning women in Corinth. History tells us that the Gentile women as a class were kept ignorant, and in Corinth, the men were scarcely better:

"The church at Corinth was a vexing problem to [Paul] because of its instability. Since it was largely composed of Gentiles who had no training in the Old Testament Scriptures, and whose religious and moral antecedents were the exact opposite of Christian principle, much teaching was required to bring them up to the place of spiritual maturity (1 Cor. 3:1-3)."[2]

Neither Male Nor Female: Just Folks

*For ye are all the children of God by faith in Christ Jesus. For as many of you as have been baptized **into Christ** have put on Christ. There is neither Jew nor Greek, there is neither bond nor free, **there is neither male nor female: for ye are all one in Christ Jesus.** And if ye be Christ's, then **are ye Abraham's seed, and heirs** according to the promise (Galatians 3:26-29).*

When it comes to the Church, when it comes to spiritual things, when it comes to the Body of Christ, *there are no distinctions between men and women.* As far as God is concerned, "...ye are all one in Christ Jesus" (Gal. 3:28). We're "just folks."

This is where, in my opinion, many have missed it. They've made it a "man and woman" proposition, when it is not. It is a "husband and wife" proposition. The man is not the head of the woman in the Church, but the husband is the head of the wife in the home. The solution to our problem doesn't stop there, however. We will only come into the fullness of God's plan if we dig a little deeper into God's Word to discover just what it means for a man to be "the head of the woman" in the Creator's way of thinking. (We may be in for a shock....)

*Giving thanks always for all things unto God and the Father in the name of our Lord Jesus Christ; submitting yourselves **one to another** in the fear of God. Wives, submit yourselves **unto your own husbands,*** *as unto the Lord. For **the husband is the head of the wife, even as Christ is the head of the church:** and He is the saviour of the body. Therefore **as the church is subject unto Christ, so let the wives be to their own husbands** in every thing* (Ephesians 5:20-24).

These verses from Paul's letter to the Ephesian believers describe the central focus of this book. But the verses that follow reveal the true *context* and spirit of love behind Paul's comments. It is this larger picture, which includes the husband's grave responsibilities as being even more weighty than those of the submissive wife, that brings peace and security to everyone involved in this "debate." In Paul's mind, the marriage relationship perfectly pictured the relationship of the submitted Church, the Bride of Christ, to her Lord and Savior, Jesus. We must understand the one to understand and better appreciate the other. Look closely at what Paul says to husbands in particular:

*Husbands, love your wives, even as Christ also loved the church, and gave Himself for it; that He might sanctify and cleanse it with the washing of water by the word, that He might present it to Himself a glorious church, not having spot, or wrinkle, or any such thing; but that it should be holy and without blemish. **So ought men to love their wives as their own bodies. He that loveth his wife loveth himself.** For no man ever yet hated his own flesh; but nourisheth and cherisheth it, even as the Lord the church: for we are members of His body, of His flesh, and of His bones. For this cause shall a man leave his father and mother, and shall be joined unto his wife, and they two shall be one flesh. **This is a*** *great mystery: but I speak concerning Christ and the church. Nevertheless let every one of you in particular so love his wife even as himself; and the wife see that she reverence her husband. Children, obey your parents in the Lord: for this is right. Honour thy father and mother; which is the first commandment with promise; that it may be well with thee, and thou mayest live long on the earth. And, ye fathers, provoke not your children to wrath: but bring them up in the nurture and admonition of the Lord* (Ephesians 5:25–6:4).

Let me say that if the Church ever understands and applies this passage from Ephesians, then the subject of "submission" and the roles of the genders in Church life and ministry will become "non-issues" overnight!

How can I say such a thing? It is *easy* to submit to Jesus Christ because He sacrificed Himself to reaffirm our eternal value and precious worth. In the same way, a husband is *commanded* to love his wife and give himself for her just as Christ loves the Church and gave Himself for it! Whenever that happens, wives will find it *easy* to submit to their loving husbands! (And husbands will find it difficult to misuse, abuse, or otherwise mistreat their wives when they have paid such a high price of self-sacrifice and tender affection for them.) The same holds true for children in a godly home where both parents walk in submission to one another.

Submission Is for Everybody

Ephesians chapter 5 is Paul's great ode to the Christ-centered family life. The subject of "submission" is for *everybody*, not just for women and children. The subject of "headship" is for *everybody*, not just for women and children. If we consider Paul's command to members of the Church that we "submit ourselves one to another" (see Eph. 5:21), that means that, when appropriate, men are to submit themselves to their wives, and parents will (when appropriate) submit their wills to the counsel or wishes of their children! (Anyone can be "right" once in awhile! And anyone can be wrong once in awhile too! And the greatest among us can learn from the least among us, as long as we retain a "teachable spirit.")

If you recall, Paul instructed the church leaders at Rome to "receive" and "assist" a woman named Phebe. His wording was very strong in its context, bordering on the very meaning of "submit"! This is a classic example of us submitting one to another in humility and honor for one another:

*I commend unto you Phebe our sister, which is a servant of the church which is at Cenchrea: that ye receive her in the Lord, as becometh saints, and **that ye assist her in whatsoever business she hath need of you**: for she hath been a succourer of many, and of myself also* (Romans 16:1-2).

Then the apostle went on to name a husband-wife team that is prominent in the Book of Acts. Oddly enough, in every mention of this couple, Paul mentions the wife, Priscilla, *first*. This was considered improper in Middle Eastern society (and even in our day) unless there were compelling reasons for it. Paul met Priscilla first in his ministry, and evidently this woman carried a strong anointing in her life, along with her husband, Aquila:

*Greet Priscilla and Aquila my helpers in Christ Jesus: who have for my life **laid down their own necks**: unto whom not only I give thanks, but also all*

the churches of the Gentiles. Likewise **greet the
church that is in their house.** *Salute my wellbeloved
Epaenetus, who is the firstfruits of Achaia unto
Christ. Greet* **Mary, who bestowed much labour on
us.** *Salute Andronicus and Junia, my kinsmen, and
my fellowprisoners, who are of note among the apostles, who also were in Christ before me* (Romans
16:3-7).

Jesus gave Himself for the Church because He *valued*
His Bride, His Church, enough to lay down His very life for
her—even though at the time she didn't exist, and her members (you and I) were totally unworthy of His love and sacrifice! Indeed, the Word says, "While we were yet sinners,
Christ died for us" (Rom. 5:8b).

There is another special situation addressed by Peter that
should not be neglected when discussing the topic of
women and submission. This is the case of women married
to unsaved husbands. Peter's counsel is remarkable, particularly if we examine it using Weymouth's clear translation
of the passage from Peter's first Epistle:

*Married women, in the same way, be submissive to
your husbands,* **so that even if some of them disbe-
lieve the Word, they may, apart from the Word, be
won over by the daily life of their wives, after seeing
their daily lives so chaste and reverent.** *Yours ought
not to be the outward adornment of platting the hair,
putting on jewels of gold, or wearing various dresses,* **but an inward beauty of nature, the imperish-
able ornament of a peaceful and gentle spirit,** *which
is indeed precious in the sight of God. For this is how
of old the holy women, who set their hopes upon God*

*used to adorn themselves, being submissive to their husbands. Thus, Sarah obeyed Abraham, calling him master. And you have become Sarah's children if you do right and permit nothing whatever to terrify you. Husbands, in the same way, live with your wives with the clear recognition of the fact that they are weaker than you. Yet, **since you are heirs with them** of God's free gift of life, **treat them with honor: so your prayers be unrestrained*** (1 Peter 3:1-7 Weymouth).

One of the great secrets of the Kingdom of God is the fact that "power" and strength aren't always found where we think they should be. Peter makes it clear that a wife has great power in her husband's life, and that it is by her godly, loving life of faith that she will win over her husband—not through constant nagging, haranguing, or badgering with quoted Scripture or self-righteous accusations.

A submitted life is not necessarily a powerless life. David was submitted to the authority of King Saul throughout the years he spent running for his life in the wilderness of Engedi, but he was not powerless. By his careful obedience to God and respect for authority (even when the one wielding the authority didn't seem to deserve that respect), David went through life "with God on his side."

Both men and women in God's Kingdom need to learn this same valuable truth and live by it. We look to Peter once again to sum up the matter of submission in the home and the Body of Christ:

Likewise, ye younger, submit yourselves unto the elder. Yea, all of you be subject one to another, and be clothed with humility: for God resisteth the proud, and giveth grace to the humble. Humble yourselves therefore under the mighty hand of God, that He may exalt you in due time: casting all your care upon Him; for He careth for you (1 Peter 5:5-7).

This word was written in the continuing context of submitting one to another, and the apostle Peter—who was perhaps the most proud and quick-tempered of all the disciples of Jesus Christ—demonstrates that he had come through the fire of testing and trial and emerged with pure gold in his heart and demeanor. It is the impetuous Peter who tells us to humble ourselves under the mighty hand of God. We desperately need to listen to him today, whether we are male or female, young or old, married or single, rich or poor. We all serve one God who demands that we have humble hearts and walk in submission and respect one for another.

What about the woman? We need to release every woman in the Body of Christ to be everything God intends for her to be! Jesus didn't lay down His life for the Church to "keep her under His foot." No! He died so that she (and we) might live the abundant life! It pleased Him to raise us (the Church, the Body, the Bride) up *with Him* to rule and to reign with Him in glory! Shouldn't we take this same attitude and aim as our own?

It is time to release the immeasurable wealth of love, encouragement, ministry, and potential that God has deposited in the women of the Church. This can only be done as we take practical, tangible steps to encourage and release women to fulfill their callings with the blessing and encouragement of the entire Church. May God be well pleased as we receive and honor one another, even as we honor Him in our midst.

We will be the richer for it....

Endnotes

1. Let me clarify that these women were not stupid or lacking in intelligence. They were simply unlearned and untaught, and they didn't possess the knowledge to understand certain things without simplification and restatement by others better trained than they.

2. Merrill C. Tenney, *New Testament Survey* (Grand Rapids, MI: Wm. B. Eerdmans Publishing Co., 1972), 294.

Exciting titles
by T.D. Jakes

CAN YOU STAND TO BE BLESSED?

You ask God to bless you and difficulties arise. Why? This book will release the hidden strength within you to go on in God, fulfilling the destiny He has for you. The way to this success is full of twists and turns, yet you can make it through to incredible blessing in your life. The only question left will be, *Can You Stand to Be Blessed?*
ISBN 1-56043-801-0 $9.99p

CAN YOU STAND TO BE BLESSED? WORKBOOK
ISBN 1-56043-812-6 $7.99p

NAKED AND NOT ASHAMED

With a powerful anointing, Bishop T.D. Jakes challenges us to go below the surface and become completely and honestly vulnerable before God and man. In relationships, in prayer, in ministry—we need to be willing to be open and transparent. Why do we fear? God already knows us, but He cannot heal our hidden hurts unless we expose them to Him. Only then can we be *Naked and Not Ashamed*!
ISBN 1-56043-835-5 $9.99p

NAKED AND NOT ASHAMED WORKBOOK
ISBN 1-56043-259-4 $7.99p

WOMAN, THOU ART LOOSED!

This book offers healing to hurting single mothers, insecure women, and battered wives; and hope to abused girls and women in crisis! Hurting women around the nation—and those who minister to them—are devouring the compassionate truths in Bishop T.D. Jakes' *Woman, Thou Art Loosed!*
ISBN 1-56043-100-8 $9.99p

WOMAN, THOU ART LOOSED! WORKBOOK
ISBN 1-56043-810-X $7.99p

Available at your local Christian bookstore.
Internet: http://www.reapernet.com